# Stuffed
## COOKIES&
## CUPCAKES

D0047985

Printed in the United States of America
by G&R Publishing Co.

Distributed By:

507 Industrial Street
Waverly, IA 50677

ISBN-13: 978-1-56383-431-8
ISBN-10: 1-56383-431-6
Item #7077

# For Stuffed Cookie and Cupcake Magic:

 When specified in the recipe, chill the dough for easier handling and to provide a firmer texture.

 Be sure your cookies' fillings are covered completely to help them stay snugly inside where they belong.

 Unless otherwise noted, line baking sheets with parchment paper. It can be reused when baking multiple batches of the same cookies and then thrown away when you're done, making clean-up a breeze.

 For best results, bake each batch of cookies on a cool baking sheet.

 To get results like the pictures inside, follow directions in the recipes; however, don't be afraid to experiment. Sometimes you find your favorite new recipe that way.

 Some of the recipes make small batches. Feel free to double them if you'd like; these stuffed treats will go fast!

**Get ready for some immensely fun, intensely sweet, double-decker deliciousness.**

# Candy Bar Stuffs

## Ingredients

¾ C. butter,
   melted and cooled

1 C. brown sugar

½ C. sugar

1 T. clear vanilla extract

2 eggs

2 C. flour

½ tsp. baking soda

36 Fun Size Butterfinger
   candy bars,* unwrapped,
   plus extra for garnish,
   optional

Frosting**

# Directions

Preheat oven to 325°. Coat mini muffin pans with nonstick cooking spray; set aside. In a large mixing bowl, beat together butter, brown sugar, sugar and vanilla on medium speed until light and fluffy. Add eggs and beat until well combined.

In a medium bowl, stir together flour and baking soda; add to butter mixture, beating on low speed until just incorporated. Divide batter evenly among prepared muffin pans, filling each liner about ½ full. Set a candy bar horizontally on top of each, pushing partway into batter. Bake for 6 to 8 minutes or until golden brown. Remove from oven and set pans on wire racks for 10 minutes; then transfer cookies to racks.

Frost as desired and garnish with extra candy bars, crushed, if you'd like.

\* Or try mini dark chocolate mint cups.

\*\* Whipped White Buttercream, page 60

# Oatmeal Cream Grahamys

## Ingredients

- 1 (8 oz.) pkg. cream cheese, softened
- ¾ C. sugar, divided
- 4 tsp. clear vanilla extract, divided
- 1 C. butter, softened
- 1½ C. brown sugar
- 2 T. ground cinnamon, divided

- 3 eggs
- 2 C. finely crushed graham crackers
- 1½ C. flour
- 2½ C. quick-cooking rolled oats
- 1 tsp. baking soda
- ½ tsp. salt

# Directions

makes 36 cookies

In a small bowl, blend cream cheese, ¼ cup sugar and 2 teaspoons vanilla until well mixed; refrigerate until needed.

Preheat oven to 350°. Line baking sheets with parchment paper and set aside. In a large mixing bowl, beat together butter, brown sugar, remaining ½ cup sugar and 1 tablespoon cinnamon on medium-high speed until creamy. Add eggs and remaining 2 teaspoons vanilla, beating until well blended.

In another large bowl, stir together cracker crumbs, flour, oats, baking soda, salt and remaining 1 tablespoon cinnamon. Gradually add to butter mixture, beating until combined. Shape dough into balls about 1½" in diameter. Make a deep well in the center of each dough ball and place about 1 teaspoon chilled cream cheese mixture in each. Press dough around filling until completely covered. Transfer to a tray or pan and place in freezer for 5 minutes.

Arrange chilled dough balls on prepared baking sheets. Bake for 11 to 13 minutes or until golden brown. Let set about 2 minutes; then transfer cookies to wire racks.

# Cherry-Chocolate Kisses

## Ingredients

1 (15.25 oz.) pkg. cherry chip cake mix

Eggs, vegetable oil and water as directed on cake mix package

50 dark chocolate Hershey's Kisses, unwrapped, plus extra for garnish, optional

Frosting*

Maraschino cherries, drained, optional

# Directions

makes 50 mini cupcakes

Preheat oven to 350°. Line mini muffin pans with paper liners; set aside. In a large bowl, combine cake mix, eggs, vegetable oil and water as directed on cake mix package. Fill prepared muffin cups ½ to ⅔ full with batter and press one chocolate Kiss down into the center of each. Bake for 8 to 11 minutes or until a toothpick inserted near edge comes out clean. Transfer cupcakes to wire racks to cool completely.

Frost as desired. Grate extra Kisses and sprinkle on top of frosting or top each with a cherry, if you'd like.

* Chocolate-Cherry Frosting, page 60

# Mixed-Up Cookie Cakes

## Ingredients

1 (17.5 oz.) pkg. peanut butter cookie mix

Eggs and vegetable oil as directed on cookie mix package

21 Reese's Peanut Butter Cups

1 (18.3 oz.) pkg. fudge brownie mix

Eggs, vegetable oil and water as directed on brownie mix package

# Directions

makes 21 cookie cakes

Coat standard muffin pans with nonstick cooking spray; set aside. Blend cookie mix, eggs and vegetable oil as directed on cookie mix package. Place about 1 tablespoon dough into each of 21 prepared muffin cups, flattening dough against bottom;* place one peanut butter cup, narrow side up, in the center of each.

Mix brownie mix, eggs, vegetable oil and water as directed on browie mix package. Spread about 2 tablespoons mixture over each peanut butter cup until candy is covered. Bake for 18 minutes or until a toothpick inserted near edge comes out clean. Set pans on wire racks for 20 to 30 minutes; then run a knife around the edge of each to loosen. Let cool completely before removing from pans.

* You'll have extra cookie dough.

# Whoop-de-Doodle Snickerdoodles

## Ingredients

3 T. plus 1½ C. sugar, divided

1½ tsp. ground cinnamon, divided

½ C. vegetable shortening

½ C. butter, softened

2 eggs

2 tsp. vanilla extract

2¾ C. flour

2 tsp. cream of tartar

1 tsp. baking soda

½ tsp. salt

48 Hershey's Bliss white chocolate candies,* unwrapped

# Directions

makes 24 cookies

In a small bowl, mix 3 tablespoons sugar and 1 teaspoon cinnamon; set aside.

In a large mixing bowl, combine vegetable shortening, butter, eggs, vanilla and remaining 1½ cups sugar. Blend on medium speed until light and fluffy.

In a medium bowl, stir together flour, cream of tartar, baking soda, salt and remaining ½ teaspoon cinnamon. Add to butter mixture, beating on medium speed until well mixed. Refrigerate for at least 1 hour.

Preheat oven to 350°. For each cookie, roll one heaping tablespoon dough into a ball. Make a deep well in the center and insert two candies. Press dough together to seal. Roll in set-aside cinnamon/sugar mixture and arrange on an ungreased baking sheet. Bake for 12 minutes or until edges are golden brown. Let cool on baking sheet about 3 minutes before transferring cookies to wire racks.

* Or try Dove caramel milk chocolate candies.

# White Choco-Cherry Blast

## Ingredients

½ C. sugar, plus extra for rolling

½ C. butter, softened

6 T. brown sugar

1 egg

½ tsp. vanilla extract

1¾ C. flour

½ tsp. baking soda

½ tsp. ground cinnamon

¼ tsp. salt

1 (2 oz.) pkg. macadamia nuts, finely chopped

½ C. white chocolate chips, chopped

25 maraschino cherries, patted dry and stems removed

# Directions

Preheat oven to 350°. Line baking sheets with parchment paper and place some sugar in a small bowl; set aside.

In a large mixing bowl, beat together butter, brown sugar and remaining ½ cup sugar on high speed until smooth. Beat in egg and vanilla until well blended.

In a small bowl, stir together flour, baking soda, cinnamon and salt. Gradually add to butter mixture, blending on medium speed until well combined. Stir in nuts and white chocolate chips. For each cookie, roll 1 tablespoon dough into a ball. Make a deep well in the center of each and insert a cherry. Press dough around cherry to completely cover. Roll in set-aside sugar and arrange on prepared baking sheets. Bake for 10 to 15 minutes or until golden brown. Let cool on baking sheets for 3 minutes before removing cookies to wire racks.

# Donut-Dunked Coffee Cups

## Ingredients

1 (15.25 oz.) pkg. yellow cake mix

Eggs, vegetable oil and half the water directed on cake mix package

Brewed coffee in place of half the water directed on package

24 chocolate-covered mini donuts*

Frosting**

# Directions

makes 24 cupcakes

Preheat oven to 350°. Line standard muffin pans with paper liners; set aside. In a large mixing bowl, combine cake mix, eggs, vegetable oil, half the water directed on cake mix package and brewed coffee. Place one tablespoon batter into each prepared muffin cup; push one mini donut into batter. Add more batter, filling each liner ⅔ to ¾ full. Bake for 15 to 17 minutes or until a toothpick inserted near edge comes out clean. Cool in pan for 15 minutes before transferring cupcakes to wire racks to cool completely.

Frost as desired.

\* Or try cinnamon-sugar donut holes.

\*\* Mocha Buttercream, page 61

# Choco-Raz
# DelightFULS

## Ingredients

½ (8 oz.) pkg. cream cheese, softened

¼ C. plus 1 T. powdered sugar

2 tsp. raspberry jam

Red food coloring

1 C. flour

⅓ C. unsweetened cocoa powder

¼ tsp. baking powder

¼ tsp. salt

½ C. butter, softened

¾ C. sugar, plus extra for rolling

1 egg

½ tsp. vanilla extract

½ tsp. raspberry flavoring

# Directions

In a small bowl, stir together cream cheese, powdered sugar, jam and food coloring until well blended; cover and refrigerate until needed. In a medium bowl, stir together flour, cocoa powder, baking powder and salt; set aside.

In a large mixing bowl, mix butter and ¾ cup sugar on medium-high speed until light and fluffy. Beat in egg, vanilla and raspberry flavoring. Reduce speed to low and add flour mixture, beating until incorporated. Increase speed to medium and beat until well blended. Cover and refrigerate for 45 minutes.

Preheat oven to 350°. Line a baking sheet with parchment paper and put extra sugar in a small bowl; set aside. Roll cookie dough into 1½″ balls and flatten to about ¼″ thickness. Place one teaspoon chilled cream cheese mixture in the center of each. Fold one side of dough over filling and pinch edges together; gently roll into a ball and roll in set-aside sugar. Arrange balls on prepared baking sheet. Bake for 10 to 13 minutes or until set. Cool on pan for 15 minutes; then transfer to a clean pan and refrigerate for 30 minutes.

# Caramel-Spiked Apple Os

## Ingredients

½ C. sugar, plus extra for rolling

½ C. butter, softened

¼ tsp. salt

½ (7.4 oz.) box spiced apple cider instant drink mix

1 egg

½ tsp. vanilla extract

½ tsp. baking soda

¼ tsp. baking powder

1½ C. flour

20 Werther's Soft Creme Caramels

# Directions

makes 20 cookies

Preheat oven to 350°. Line baking sheets with parchment paper and put extra sugar in a small bowl; set aside.

In a large mixing bowl, beat together butter, ½ cup sugar, salt and drink mix on medium speed until light and fluffy. Add egg and vanilla, mixing until well blended.

In a small bowl, stir together baking soda, baking powder and flour. Add to butter mixture, beating on medium speed until combined. For each cookie, roll one level measuring tablespoon dough into a ball and push one caramel into the center. Press dough around caramel until completely covered; dip in set-aside sugar and arrange on prepared baking sheets, sugared side up. Bake for 12 to 14 minutes or until edges are golden brown. Slide parchment paper and cookies from baking sheets; set aside to cool.

# Peanut Butter Cookie Buttons

## Ingredients

2 oz. unsweetened
   baking chocolate

1½ C. plus 2 T. flour

½ tsp. baking soda

½ tsp. salt

1½ tsp. vanilla extract

½ C. half & half

½ C. butter, softened

1 C. brown sugar

1 egg

34 mini Nutter Butter
   cookies

Frosting*

# Directions

makes 34 cookies

Preheat oven to 350°. Line baking sheets with parchment paper. In a small microwave-safe bowl, melt chocolate according to package directions; stir until smooth. In another small bowl, sift together flour, baking soda and salt. In a separate small bowl, stir together vanilla and half & half; set all aside.

In a large mixing bowl, beat together butter and brown sugar on medium speed until light and fluffy. Add egg and blend well. Stir in melted chocolate. Alternately add flour mixture and half & half mixture, beating until combined. Drop by rounded teaspoonfuls on prepared baking sheets. Top each with a Nutter Butter and press gently. Place one rounded teaspoon dough on top, covering Nutter Butter completely; press edges together gently. Bake for 10 to 12 minutes. Remove from oven and let cool on baking sheets for 2 minutes before transferring cookies to wire racks to cool completely.

Frost as desired.

* Peanut Butter Frosting, page 61

# Joy-Filled Brownie Babies

## Ingredients

½ C. sweetened condensed milk

1¼ C. sweetened flaked coconut, plus extra for garnish, optional

¼ C. powdered sugar

1 (19.9 oz.) pkg. dark chocolate fudge brownie mix

Eggs, vegetable oil and water as directed on brownie mix package

⅓ C. dark chocolate chips

55 unsalted almonds

Frosting*

# Directions

makes 55 mini cupcakes

Preheat oven to 350°. Line mini muffin pans with paper liners; set aside. In a small bowl, stir together sweetened condensed milk, 1¼ cups coconut and powdered sugar; set aside.

In a large mixing bowl, blend brownie mix, eggs, vegetable oil and water as directed on brownie mix package. Stir in chocolate chips. Place one measuring teaspoonful of brownie batter into each prepared muffin cup. Add ½ teaspoon coconut mixture and 1 almond. Top with one measuring teaspoon brownie batter. Bake for 8 to 10 minutes or until a toothpick inserted near center comes out clean. Transfer to wire racks to cool completely.

Frost as desired and sprinkle with extra coconut, if you'd like.

* Chocolate Glaze, recipe page 62

# Stuffed Ranger Round-Ups

## Ingredients

¼ C. creamy peanut butter

¼ C. butter, softened

6 T. brown sugar

¼ C. sugar

1 egg

½ tsp. vanilla extract

¼ tsp. baking soda

½ tsp. salt

½ C. plus 1 T. flour

1 C. quick-cooking rolled oats

½ C. butterscotch chips

½ C. Rice Krispies cereal

14 mini Snickers candy bars, unwrapped

# Directions

Preheat oven to 350°. Line a baking sheet with parchment paper; set aside. In a large mixing bowl, beat together peanut butter, butter, brown sugar and sugar until well blended. Add egg and vanilla; beat until light and fluffy.

In a small bowl, stir together baking soda, salt, flour and oats. Add to peanut butter mixture, blending until just combined. Stir in butterscotch chips and cereal. For each cookie, drop by level measuring tablespoonful on prepared baking sheet. Set a candy bar horizontally on top and press gently. Place one level tablespoon dough on top of candy and press edges together to seal. Bake for 12 minutes or until light golden brown. Cool on pan for 5 minutes before transferring cookies to wire racks.

# Party-in-Every-Bite Cupcakes

## Ingredients

1 (9 oz.) pkg. white cake mix

Egg and water as directed on cake mix package

1 T. decorating sprinkles, plus extra for decorating, optional

1 (15.6 oz.) tub white confetti frosting

1 (18.25 oz.) pkg. chocolate cake mix

1 C. sour cream

½ C. vegetable oil

4 eggs

1 tsp. vanilla extract

# Directions

makes 24 cupcakes

Mix white cake mix, egg and water as directed on cake mix package. Stir in 1 tablespoon decorating sprinkles. Bake in any size pan as directed on package and let cool.

Crumble cooled cake into a large bowl. Add ¼ tub frosting and its entire package of confetti sprinkles. Stir until well blended. Roll mixture into 24 balls; set aside.

Preheat oven to 350°. Line standard muffin pans with paper liners; set aside. In a large mixing bowl, blend chocolate cake mix, sour cream, vegetable oil, eggs, vanilla and ½ cup water at low speed until incorporated. Increase speed to medium and beat for 2 minutes or until well blended. Place 1 tablespoon batter into each prepared muffin cup; place one set-aside cake ball on top. Top each with 1 tablespoon batter, covering cake ball. Bake for 18 to 22 minutes or until a toothpick inserted near edge comes out clean; let cool completely.

Frost as desired with remaining frosting from tub. Decorate with extra sprinkles, if you'd like.

# Chipper Studs
# & Oreo STUFF

## Ingredients

½ C. butter, softened

6 T. brown sugar

½ C. sugar

1 egg

1½ tsp. vanilla extract

1¾ C. flour

½ tsp. salt

½ tsp. baking soda

1 C. mini chocolate chips

45 mini Oreo cookies

# Directions

makes 45 cookies

Preheat oven to 350°. Line baking sheets with parchment paper; set aside. In a large mixing bowl, cream together butter, brown sugar and sugar until light and fluffy. Add egg and vanilla, mixing until well combined.

In a small bowl, stir together flour, salt and baking soda. Slowly add to butter mixture, beating until just combined. Stir in chocolate chips. For each cookie, place one packed level teaspoon dough on prepared baking sheets. Top with an Oreo and press gently. Place one packed level teaspoon dough on top and press edges together to seal. Bake for 10 to 12 minutes or until cookies are lightly browned. Let cool on pans for 5 minutes before transferring cookies to wire racks to cool. Use a cool pan to bake each remaining batch.

# Loaded Lime Cupcakes

## Ingredients

1 (6 oz.) pkg. Pepperidge Farm Lemon cookies

1 T. brown sugar

6 T. butter, melted

1 (8 oz.) pkg. cream cheese, softened

¾ C. sugar, divided

1 egg

5½ T. lime zest, divided

¼ C. plus 2 T. lime juice, divided

Green food coloring

1 (15.25 oz.) pkg. French vanilla cake mix

Eggs, vegetable oil and water as directed on cake mix package

1 C. heavy cream, chilled

# Directions

Preheat oven to 350°. Line standard muffin pans with paper liners; set aside. In a food processor, process cookies and brown sugar until finely crushed. Add butter and pulse until well blended. Press 1½ teaspoons mixture into each prepared muffin cup; set aside remaining crumb mixture.

In a small mixing bowl, blend cream cheese and ¼ cup sugar on high speed until well combined. Beat in egg, 2½ tablespoons lime zest, ¼ cup lime juice and food coloring; set aside.

In a large mixing bowl, combine cake mix, eggs, vegetable oil and water as directed on cake mix package; stir in 1½ tablespoons lime zest. Fill prepared muffin cups ½ full with batter. Place about 1 tablespoon set-aside cream cheese mixture into the center of each, pushing down slightly into batter. Bake for 15 to 18 minutes or until light golden brown. Remove from pans and cool completely.

In a medium mixing bowl, combine cream, remaining ½ cup sugar, 1½ teaspoons lime zest and remaining 2 tablespoons lime juice. Beat on high speed until stiff peaks form. Pipe whipped cream mixture on cupcakes. Sprinkle with set-aside crumbs and remaining 1 tablespoon lime zest, if you'd like.

# PB&J Pies

## Ingredients

1 (14.1 oz.) pkg.
  refrigerated pie crusts

About ⅓ (16.5 oz.) pkg.
  refrigerated peanut butter
  cookie dough, unwrapped

8 tsp. grape, strawberry
  or raspberry jelly

Sugar for sprinkling

# Directions

Let pie crusts set at room temperature for
15 minutes. Meanwhile, preheat oven to 475° and
spray a rimmed baking sheet lightly with nonstick
cooking spray. Unwrap one pie crust and unroll on
a lightly floured work surface. Using a 3½″ round
cookie cutter, cut eight rounds, rerolling and cutting
scraps as necessary. Arrange rounds on prepared
baking sheet. Cut eight ¼″ to ⅜″ slices from cookie
dough, and place one slice on the center of each pie
crust round, rounding edges of cookie dough slightly.
Place one teaspoon jelly on the center of each cookie
dough slice.

Unwrap remaining pie crust, unroll and cut as
before. Wet edges of one pie crust round on baking
sheet with water; place one of the remaining pie
crust rounds on top, edges even. Press around
edges with tines of a fork to seal tightly. Repeat
with remaining pie crust rounds. Brush top of
each with water and sprinkle with sugar. Bake for
10 to 12 minutes or until golden brown. Transfer
pies to a wire rack.

# Stuff S'more Cookies

## Ingredients

2 (1.55 oz.) Hershey's milk chocolate candy bars

8 regular marshmallows

½ C. butter, softened

¼ C. brown sugar

½ C. sugar

1 egg

1 tsp. vanilla extract

1⅓ C. flour

¾ C. finely crushed graham crackers

1 tsp. baking powder

¼ tsp. salt

# Directions

makes 16 cookies

Preheat oven to 350°. Line a baking sheet with parchment paper, break candy bars along score lines and cut marshmallows in half lengthwise; set all aside. In a large mixing bowl, beat together butter, brown sugar and sugar on medium speed until light and fluffy. Add egg and vanilla; beat until blended.

In a small bowl, stir together flour, cracker crumbs, baking powder and salt. Add to butter mixture, a little at a time, mixing on low speed until combined. For each cookie, use one rounded tablespoon dough; divide in half to create two cookie dough mounds. On prepared baking sheet, stack one dough mound, two chocolate candy rectangles, one marshmallow half and another dough mound. Squeeze together gently, sealing edges, so marshmallow and chocolate are completely covered. Repeat with remaining dough, candy and marshmallows. Bake for 12 to 15 minutes or until lightly browned and puffy. Transfer to waxed paper to cool. Best if served the same day they're made.

# I Spy Banana Cream Pie

## Ingredients

1½ C. milk

1 (3 oz.) pkg. banana cream or vanilla cook & serve pudding mix

1 (14.1 oz.) pkg. refrigerated pie crusts at room temperature, unwrapped

1 (15.25 oz.) pkg. devil's food cake mix

Eggs, vegetable oil and water as directed on cake mix package

Whipped topping, thawed

Chocolate curls, optional

# Directions

Coat mini muffin pans with nonstick cooking spray and line standard muffin pans with paper liners; set aside. In a small saucepan, combine milk and half the pudding mix, saving remainder for another use. Cook over medium heat until mixture boils, stirring constantly; remove from heat, transfer to a small bowl, place plastic wrap directly on surface and refrigerate.

Preheat oven to 375°. Unroll pie crusts on a lightly floured work surface. Using a 2½" round cookie cutter, cut 28 rounds, rerolling and cutting scraps. Transfer rounds to prepared mini muffin cups, pressing crust against bottom and sides. Prick bottoms with tines of a fork. Bake for 10 minutes or until golden brown. Remove crusts from pans to cool.

Fill each cooled crust with chilled pudding. In a large mixing bowl, beat together cake mix, eggs, vegetable oil and water as directed on cake mix package. Place 1 heaping tablespoon batter into each prepared standard muffin cup. Set a filled pie crust into batter. Top with 1 heaping tablespoon batter, filling in around outside of crust first and then covering pudding last. Bake for 18 minutes or until toothpick inserted near edge comes out clean. Transfer cupcakes to wire racks to cool; refrigerate. Serve with whipped topping and chocolate curls, if you'd like. Best if served the same day they're made.

# Inside-Out Cookies

## Ingredients

¼ C. butter

2½ T. brown sugar

2 T. creamy peanut butter

½ tsp. vanilla extract

1½ C. plus 2 T. milk
  chocolate chips, divided

6 T. powdered sugar

1 T. flour

Pinch of salt

¼ C. mini chocolate chips

# Directions

makes 20 cookie cups

In a small saucepan, melt butter over medium heat. Add brown sugar. Whisk until brown sugar dissolves and mixture comes to a boil; boil for 1 minute, stirring constantly. Remove from heat and whisk in peanut butter and vanilla. Set aside to cool.

Line mini muffin pans with paper liners. In a small microwave-safe bowl, melt ½ cup plus 2 tablespoons milk chocolate chips according to package directions; stir until smooth. Place about 1 level measuring teaspoon melted chocolate into each prepared muffin cup. Use a small food-safe brush to coat sides of liners with chocolate until covered. Freeze for 20 minutes.

Add powdered sugar, flour and salt to cooled peanut butter mixture, stirring until dough is smooth. Fold in mini chocolate chips until thoroughly combined. Refrigerate for 15 minutes.

Roll chilled cookie dough into balls using about 1 teaspoonful of dough and place each ball into a chilled chocolate cup. Freeze for 10 minutes.

In a small microwave-safe bowl, melt remaining 1 cup milk chocolate chips and pour about 1 teaspoonful over each cookie dough ball, covering completely. Freeze for 15 minutes. These are easiest to eat when frozen or nearly frozen.

# Spiced Cream Puff Bundles

## Ingredients

2 C. cake flour

2 tsp. ground cinnamon

1 tsp. baking soda

½ tsp. salt

½ tsp. ground allspice

¼ tsp. ground ginger

¼ tsp. ground nutmeg, plus extra for sprinkling, optional

½ C. butter, softened

1½ C. brown sugar

4 eggs, separated

1 C. buttermilk

1 (14.1 oz.) pkg. frozen mini cream puffs

Frosting*

# Directions

makes 32 cupcakes

Preheat oven to 350°. Chill a medium mixing bowl and beaters. Line standard muffin pans with paper liners. In a medium bowl, sift together flour, cinnamon, baking soda, salt, allspice, ginger and ¼ teaspoon nutmeg; set all aside.

In a large mixing bowl, beat together butter on medium speed until creamy. Add brown sugar and beat until well blended. Beat in egg yolks. Alternately add flour mixture and buttermilk, beating until blended.

In chilled mixing bowl using chilled beaters, beat egg whites on high speed until stiff peaks form; fold into cupcake batter until incorporated. Fill prepared muffin cups ½ full with batter. Push one frozen cream puff down into the center of each. Bake for 15 to 18 minutes. Transfer cupcakes to wire racks to cool completely.

Frost as desired and sprinkle with extra nutmeg, if you'd like.

* Fluffy White Frosting, page 62

# Dippity-do-Wiches

## Ingredients

1 (15.25 oz.) pkg.
Double Stuf Oreos*

15 Reese's Peanut Butter
Cups, unwrapped

About 2¼ C. dark
chocolate candy wafers

# Directions

makes 15 cookies

Separate each Oreo by twisting the cookies so the filling remains on one side. Crush a few of the cookies without filling to use as garnish, if desired; set aside. Save remaining unfilled cookies for another use.

Place one peanut butter cup on the filling side of half the cookies; set remaining filled cookies on top of peanut butter cups with filling against peanut butter cup. Press gently to secure.

Set a sheet of waxed paper on a flat work surface. In a medium microwave-safe bowl, melt candy wafers according to package directions; stir until smooth. Dip each filled cookie into melted chocolate wafers until coated; remove with a fork, tapping against bowl to remove excess chocolate. Set on waxed paper and sprinkle with set-aside crushed cookies, if you'd like. Let dry.

* Use chocolate, golden or a combination.

# Lemon Luscious Cookie Pies

## Ingredients

½ C. butter, softened

½ C. sugar

1 egg white

1 tsp. vanilla extract

½ tsp. lemon flavoring

1½ C. flour, plus extra
   for rolling

1 tsp. baking powder

½ tsp. salt

Coarse sugar, optional

Lemon pie filling

½ C. powdered sugar,
   optional

1 T. milk, optional

# Directions

In a large mixing bowl, beat together butter and sugar on medium speed until light and fluffy. Add egg white, vanilla and lemon flavoring, beating until smooth and creamy.

In a small bowl, stir together 1½ cups flour, baking powder and salt. Add to butter mixture, beating on medium speed until well mixed. Wrap dough in plastic wrap and refrigerate for 20 minutes.

Preheat oven to 350°. Line baking sheets with parchment paper and place coarse sugar in a small bowl; set aside. On a floured surface, roll half the dough to about ¼" thickness. Using a 2" round or ruffled cookie cutter, cut 16 cookie dough rounds; arrange on prepared baking sheets. Place ½ teaspoon pie filling on the center of each cookie dough round. Roll and cut 16 rounds from remaining cookie dough; prick with the tines of a fork, dampen one side with a bit of water and dip damp side in set-aside sugar. Wet the top edge of one cookie dough round on baking sheet with a bit of water and place one of the remaining cookie dough rounds on top, sugar side up, edges even. Press around edges with the tines of a fork, sealing in filling. Repeat with remaining rounds. Bake for 12 to 15 minutes or until set. Transfer cookies to a wire rack to cool completely.

In a small bowl, stir together powdered sugar and milk until smooth. Drizzle over cooled cookies, if you'd like.

# Berry Blasted Cupcakes

## Ingredients

1½ C. flour

1¾ tsp. baking powder

1 C. sugar

½ C. butter, softened

2 eggs

1 T. vanilla extract

½ C. half & half

12 ripe strawberries, hulled*

Frosting**

Fresh mint leaves
   for garnish, optional

# Directions

Preheat oven to 350°. Line a standard muffin pan with paper liners. In a medium bowl, stir together flour and baking powder; set aside.

In a medium mixing bowl, beat together sugar and butter until light and fluffy. Beat in eggs, one at a time. Stir in vanilla. Alternately add flour mixture and half & half, beating until mixture is smooth. Divide batter evenly among prepared muffin cups and bake for 20 to 25 minutes or until a toothpick inserted near center comes out clean. Set pan on a wire rack for 10 minutes; then transfer cupcakes to rack to cool completely.

Cut and remove a cone-shaped piece from the top of each cooled cupcake approximately the size of a strawberry. Set one strawberry in each cupcake cavity; then cover lightly and refrigerate for 15 minutes.

Frost as desired and garnish with mint leaves, if you'd like.

\* Cut and remove a thin slice from the top of each berry, if needed.

\*\* Strawberry Icing, page 62

# Peppermint Treasures

## Ingredients

1½ C. flour

¼ C. unsweetened
  cocoa powder

½ C. sugar

¼ C. brown sugar

1 tsp. salt

½ tsp. baking soda

¾ C. butter, melted

1 egg

½ tsp. peppermint flavoring

24 mini peppermint patties,
  unwrapped and chilled

1 C. white chocolate chips

# Directions

makes 24 cookies

In a large mixing bowl, combine flour, cocoa powder, sugar, brown sugar, salt and baking soda. Beat in butter, egg and peppermint flavoring on low speed until well blended. Transfer mixture to a piece of plastic wrap; flatten dough, wrap in plastic and refrigerate for 30 minutes.

Preheat oven to 350°. Line two baking sheets with parchment paper. Place ½ tablespoon dough on prepared baking sheet, flatten and set a peppermint patty in the center. Cover with ½ tablespoon dough, flatten and press sides of both dough pieces around peppermint patty until completely covered. Repeat with remaining dough and peppermint patties. Smooth top of dough with fingertips. Bake for 12 to 15 minutes or until set. Transfer parchment paper with cookies to wire racks to cool completely.

In a small microwave-safe bowl, melt white chocolate chips according to package directions; stir until smooth. Transfer melted white chocolate to a small zippered plastic bag. Cut a tiny corner from bag and drizzle white chocolate over cooled cookies; let set until dry.

# Coconut Surprise

## Ingredients

¼ tsp. baking soda

1 tsp. baking powder

Dash of salt

1¼ C. flour

6 T. butter, softened

½ C. plus 2 T. sugar

1 egg plus 1 egg white

½ tsp. clear vanilla extract

½ tsp. coconut flavoring

⅔ C. milk

30 Ferrero Rafaello or Garden candies

½ C. sweetened flaked coconut, toasted

Frosting*

makes 30 mini cupcakes

# Directions

Preheat oven to 350°. Line mini muffin pans with paper liners; set aside. In a medium bowl, stir together baking soda, baking powder, salt and flour.

In a large mixing bowl, combine butter and sugar on medium-high speed until light and fluffy. Add egg, egg white, vanilla and coconut flavoring. Alternately add flour mixture and milk, beating until well combined. Place one level tablespoon batter into each prepared muffin cup; push one candy into the center of each. Bake for 13 minutes or until cupcakes are golden brown; remove from pans and let cool completely.

Frost as desired. Sprinkle lightly with toasted coconut.

\* Coconut-Cream Cheese Frosting, page 63

Try other Ferrero candies, such as Rocher or Rond Noir for a chocolate surprise center.

# Salty-Sweet Cookie Treats

## Ingredients

½ C. Nutella hazelnut spread

1¾ C. sugar, divided

2½ C. flour

½ tsp. baking powder

½ tsp. salt

¾ C. plus 2T. butter, softened

2 eggs

2 tsp. vanilla extract

1 T. sea salt

# Directions

makes 24 cookies

Line a baking sheet with parchment paper. Using a 1 teaspoon measuring spoon, place Nutella in small mounds on prepared baking sheet. Place in the freezer for 15 minutes. Place ¼ cup sugar in a small bowl. In a medium bowl, whisk together flour, baking powder and salt. Line two additional baking sheets with parchment paper. Set all aside.

Preheat oven to 350°. In a large mixing bowl, beat together butter and remaining 1½ cups sugar on medium speed until light and fluffy. Beat in eggs, one at a time. Add vanilla and beat to combine. Reduce speed to low and gradually beat in flour mixture until just combined. Slightly flatten 1 tablespoon dough and sprinkle with a bit of sea salt. Set one Nutella mound on top. Cover with 1 tablespoon dough, sealing edges. Roll into a ball and roll in set-aside sugar. Repeat with remaining dough and Nutella. Arrange on prepared baking sheets. Bake for 12 to 15 minutes or until edges are set. Set pan on wire racks for 10 minutes; then transfer cookies to racks.

# Yum-mazing
# Fudge Cookies

## Ingredients

1 (12 oz.) pkg. semi-sweet
   chocolate chips

1 (8 oz.) pkg. cream
   cheese, softened

2 C. flour

25 mini Reese's Peanut
   Butter Cups, unwrapped

1 C. white candy wafers

½ C. dark chocolate
   candy wafers

# Directions

makes 25 cookies

Preheat oven to 350°. In a medium microwave-safe bowl, melt chocolate chips according to package directions; stir until smooth. Add cream cheese, stirring to blend well. Add flour and stir or mix with your hands until well blended. Flatten about 1 tablespoon dough and place a peanut butter cup in the center. Gently wrap dough around peanut butter cup until completely covered. Roll into a ball and place on ungreased baking sheets. Bake for 10 minutes. Transfer cookies to parchment paper to cool completely.

In a small microwave-safe bowl, melt white candy wafers according to package directions; stir until smooth. Dip the top of each cooled cookie into melted white wafers and return to parchment paper to dry.

In a separate small microwave-safe bowl, melt chocolate candy wafers. Transfer melted chocolate wafers to a small zippered plastic bag. Cut a tiny corner from bag and drizzle chocolate over cookies; let set until chocolate is dry.

# Cupcake Cookie Cushions

## Ingredients

1¾ C. flour, divided

⅛ tsp. plus ½ tsp. baking soda, divided

⅛ tsp. plus ¼ tsp. salt, divided

¼ C. butter, melted

¼ C. brown sugar

2 T. plus 1 C. sugar, divided

2 T. half & half

3½ tsp. vanilla extract, divided

¾ C. mini semi-sweet chocolate chips, divided

½ C. unsweetened cocoa powder

½ C. vegetable oil

1 egg

Frosting*

# Directions

In a small bowl, stir together ¾ cup flour, ⅛ teaspoon baking soda and ⅛ teaspoon salt; set aside. In a medium bowl, beat together butter, brown sugar, 2 tablespoons sugar, half & half and 2 teaspoons vanilla. Stir in flour mixture and ½ cup chocolate chips. Refrigerate for 15 minutes. Divide dough into 12 even balls, about 1½ tablespoons each, and place on a baking sheet; freeze for 30 minutes or until firm.

Preheat oven to 375°. Line a standard muffin pan with paper liners. In a large mixing bowl, combine cocoa powder, remaining 1 cup flour, remaining 1 cup sugar, remaining ½ teaspoon baking soda and remaining ¼ teaspoon salt; blend well. Add ¾ cup hot water, vegetable oil, egg and remaining 1½ teaspoons vanilla, beating on low speed until mixed; then beat on medium-high speed for 1 minute. Divide batter evenly among prepared muffin cups. Push a frozen cookie dough ball down into the center of each until it rests on the bottom and is nearly covered with batter. Bake for 20 to 25 minutes or until a toothpick inserted near edge comes out clean. Set pan on a wire rack to cool completely.

Frost as desired and garnish with remaining ¼ cup chocolate chips.

\* Cookie Dough Frosting, page 63

# Frosting Recipes

## Whipped White Buttercream

*Shown with **Candy Bar Stuffs**, page 4*

1 C. vegetable shortening
4 C. powdered sugar
¼ tsp. salt

1 tsp. clear vanilla extract
½ tsp. butter flavoring
6 T. milk

In a large mixing bowl, beat together shortening, powdered sugar, salt, vanilla, butter flavoring and milk on low speed until incorporated. Beat on high speed for 8 to 10 minutes.

## Chocolate-Cherry Frosting

*Shown with **Cherry-Chocolate Kisses**, page 8*

¼ C. butter, softened
2 oz. unsweetened chocolate, melted and cooled

2 C. powdered sugar, sifted
3 to 4 T. maraschino cherry juice

In a medium mixing bowl, beat together butter and cooled chocolate on medium speed until blended. Reduce speed to low and beat in powdered sugar and cherry juice until combined. Beat on medium speed until light and fluffy.

# Mocha Buttercream

*Shown with **Donut-Dunked Coffee Cups**, page 16*

1½ C. butter, softened
3 C. powdered sugar
¼ C. unsweetened
    cocoa powder

2 tsp. vanilla extract
2 T. instant coffee granules

In a large mixing bowl, beat together butter and powdered sugar on medium speed until light and fluffy. Add cocoa powder and vanilla; beat until combined. In a small bowl, stir together coffee granules and a splash of hot water until dissolved. Add coffee to butter mixture and beat until combined. Beat on high speed for 2 minutes.

# Peanut Butter Frosting

*Shown with **Peanut Butter Cookie Buttons**, page 22*

½ C. creamy peanut butter
2 T. butter, softened
¼ C. half & half

½ tsp. vanilla extract
1 C. powdered sugar, sifted

In a small mixing bowl, beat together peanut butter, butter, half & half and vanilla on medium speed until well blended. Reduce speed to low and add powdered sugar. Beat until creamy, adding a little more half & half if needed for spreading consistency.

# Chocolate Glaze

*Shown with **Joy-Filled Brownie Babies**, page 24*

| | |
|---|---|
| 2 T. butter, melted | 1 C. powdered sugar, sifted |
| 2 T. unsweetened cocoa powder | ½ tsp. vanilla extract |

In a small bowl, stir together butter, cocoa powder, powdered sugar, vanilla and 2 tablespoons hot water until smooth.

# Fluffy White Frosting

*Shown with **Spiced Cream Puff Bundles**, page 42*

| | |
|---|---|
| 1 C. sugar | ½ tsp. cream of tartar |
| 3 egg whites | 1 tsp. vanilla extract |

In a large saucepan, combine sugar, egg whites, cream of tartar and 3 tablespoons water. Cook on medium-low heat, beating with an electric hand mixer until frosting reaches 160°, 10 to 15 minutes. Immediately transfer mixture to a large bowl; add vanilla and beat on high speed until frosting forms stiff peaks, 5 to 7 minutes. Note: Do not make on a humid day.

# Strawberry Icing

*Shown with **Berry Blasted Cupcakes**, page 48*

| | |
|---|---|
| ¼ C. butter, softened | ¼ tsp. clear vanilla extract |
| ¼ C. pureed strawberries | 2⅓ C. powdered sugar, sifted |
| Pinch of salt | |

In a medium bowl, beat butter on high speed until smooth. Mix in strawberries, salt and vanilla. Reduce speed to low; add powdered sugar, a little at a time, beating until blended. Beat on high speed until fluffy. Refrigerate for 15 minutes.

# Coconut-Cream Cheese Frosting

*Shown with **Coconut Surprise**, page 52*

½ (8 oz.) pkg. cream
cheese, softened
¼ C. butter, softened
2 C. powdered sugar
1 T. heavy cream

¼ tsp. salt
½ tsp. coconut flavoring
½ tsp. vanilla extract
½ C. sweetened flaked
coconut

In a medium mixing bowl, beat together cream cheese and butter on medium speed until light and fluffy. Gradually beat in powdered sugar and cream. Beat in salt, coconut flavoring and vanilla until mixture is smooth. Stir in coconut.

# Cookie Dough Frosting

*Shown with **Cupcake Cookie Cushions**, page 58*

¾ C. butter, softened
1¾ C. powdered sugar,
sifted
⅓ C. brown sugar

⅓ C. flour
1 tsp. vanilla extract

In a medium mixing bowl, beat together butter, powdered sugar and brown sugar on medium speed until smooth. Add flour and vanilla, mixing until well combined.

# Index

## Stuff my Cookies!

## Stuff my Cupcakes!

## Frost It!